ice-cold
martinis

ice-cold martinis

Ben Reed

photography by
William Lingwood

RYLAND
PETERS
& SMALL

LONDON NEW YORK

Designer **Barbara Zuñiga**
Editor **Rebecca Woods**
Production **Gordana Simakovic**
Art Director **Leslie Harrington**
Publishing Director **Alison Starling**

Mixologist **Ben Reed**
Indexer **Hilary Bird**

10 9 8 7 6 5 4 3 2 1

First published in Great Britain
in 2011
by **Ryland Peters & Small**
20–21 Jockey's Fields
London WC1R 4BW
and
Ryland Peters & Small, Inc.
519 Broadway, 5th Floor
New York NY10012

www.rylandpeters.com

The recipes in this book have been
published previously by Ryland
Peters & Small.

ISBN-13: 978-1-84975-152-0

A CIP record for this book is
available from the British Library.

Library of Congress
Cataloging-in-Publication Data

Reed, Ben.
  Ice-cold martinis / Ben Reed ;
photography by William Lingwood.
    p. cm.
  Includes index.
  ISBN 978-1-84975-152-0
1. Martinis. I. Title.
TX951.R355234 2011
641.8'74--dc22
                    2011004702

Printed in China

Note: Measurements are
occasionally given in barspoons,
which are equivalent to 5 ml or
1 teaspoon. All recipes given make
one martini.

contents

Introduction

What is a martini? To many drinkers it can only be one thing: gin and vermouth with either a lemon zest (or twist) or olive garnish. If this were the case and the boundaries for producing a martini were this rigid then we would not have the variety of 'martinis' that we enjoy today.

The argument of how best to make a martini is a redundant one. There are any number of ways to make a classic martini – all depend on personal taste (and how can that be a bad thing?). The trend of calling any drink prepared using gin or vodka as a base and served in a martini cocktail glass a 'martini' is, I think, what infuriates the purists. Just between you and me, I take secret pleasure in defying these sticklers for tradition. Indeed, I go so far as to pounce on such dinosaurs with a war cry of 'try a Cheesecake Martini on for size!' – less to influence opinion than to check that they are still awake!

I've categorized these drinks into groups to give you an idea of the differences in flavours and the ways they are made. Some require a little bit of preparation, others rely on the freshest, ripest fruit; for others still, the most delicate touch of an added ingredient is what lends the drink its individuality.

Taking ideas from cocktail bars around the world, along with a healthy smattering of my own creations, I've put together a list of martinis that should delight and amaze but, most importantly, add a little colour to the cheeks. You'll find that it's a wide-ranging collection – some you will love, some you may hate, but that's the whole fun of cocktails. There's a cocktail for everyone, and once you find it, you're well on the way to a drop of enlightenment.

Techniques

The three basic methods used to make a martini are stirring, shaking and pouring (also called the diamond method). Each method, performed correctly, has a direct effect on the character of the drink and how it appears in the glass.

Stirring
Place a barspoon into a mixing glass and fill it with ice. Stir gently in a continuous motion until the glass is cold to the touch. Add a dash of vermouth and stir (each stir should last for about 10 revolutions – try to avoid chipping the ice as this dilutes the martini) before discarding the dilution and the vermouth. Finally add the spirit and stir.

Shaking
Add the ingredients to a shaker, fill it with ice and replace the lid. Shake with strong, sharp movements (remembering to keep a hand on both parts of the shaker!). This method is useful when mixing creamy martinis.

Pouring (or diamond method)
For the coldest, purest martini – simply place a bottle of gin or vodka and your martini glasses into a freezer for 6 hours. To serve, add a dash of vermouth to a chilled glass, swill it around and discard. Pour the frozen spirit into the glass for an unadulterated cocktail.

Equipment

For a 'stirred' martini you will need a mixing glass with a strainer. A cocktail shaker is essential for those who prefer their martinis 'shaken'. One with a lid and a strainer is ideal. You will also need a measure. Modern measures are the most useful as they measure both 50 ml/2 oz. and 25 ml/1 oz. (a double and a single measure). A long handled barspoon is useful for stirring drinks and muddling fruit, herbs etc.

Garnishes

The traditional garnishes for a martini are of course an olive or a lemon zest. A certain amount of poetic licence can be used when creating garnishes for newer cocktails. Your choice of garnish should complement both the taste and the appearance of the drink. A lemon zest (or twist), properly prepared and added to the surface of a classic martini, transforms the drink. Take a sharp knife and gently skim a length of peel from the lemon – the zest should be fine with no pith. Squeeze the zest over the drink, wipe it around the rim and then drop it into the liquid. Another type of lemon garnish is the lemon peel – simply slice a thin peel from a lemon and drop it into the drink. For a flaming orange zest take a thick zest and squeeze it, skin down, over a flame and the surface of the drink (the juice from citrus fruits is flammable) then drop the zest into the martini.

Another simple and effective way to garnish your martini is to 'edge' the glass with cocoa powder, salt or nutmeg. To do this wipe a piece of orange around the rim of the glass and then place the glass face down into the powder, creating a tidy rim around the edge. Ensure that the powder does not mix directly with the martini.

classic

classic martini

This is how I would make a 'standard martini' for anyone who asked for one. While the pouring or diamond method (see page 8) is faster and the resultant drink stronger (less dilute), stirring the cocktail is a more authentic method and the original labour of love for any bartender.

a dash of vermouth (Noilly Prat or Martini Extra Dry)

75 ml/3 oz. freezing gin or vodka

an olive or a lemon twist, to garnish

Add both the ingredients to a mixing glass filled with ice and stir. Strain into a frosted martini glass and garnish with an olive or a lemon twist. Alternatively use the diamond technique.

dirty

This martini is also known as the FDR, after the man who called an end to Prohibition in the 1930s. Fittingly, the great president was an accomplished bartender who loved nothing more than flourishing his shaker for any head of state with a like mind or a dry palate.

a dash of vermouth (Noilly Prat or Martini Extra Dry)

75 ml/3 oz. freezing gin or vodka

a large dash of brine from the olive or onion jar

an olive, a lemon twist or a cocktail onion, to garnish

Add all the ingredients to a shaker filled with ice, shake sharply, and strain into a frosted martini glass. Garnish with an olive, a lemon twist or a cocktail onion.

smoky martini

This is a variation on the Dirty martini, with the whisky substituting for the olive brine, but the method is identical.

75 ml/3 oz. gin

a dash of dry vermouth

a dash of whisky

Add the gin, a dash of dry vermouth and a dash of whisky to a shaker filled with cracked ice. Shake sharply and strain into a frosted martini glass with a lemon-zested rim. Garnish with an olive.

gibson

The leading theory behind the origin of this classic martini is that it was first made at the beginning of the 20th century for Charles Gibson, a famous illustrator, at the Players Club in New York. Whatever its roots, this classic drink has truly withstood the test of time.

a dash of vermouth (Noilly Prat or Martini Extra Dry)

75 ml/3 oz. freezing gin or vodka

a cocktail onion, to garnish

Add both the ingredients to a mixing glass filled with ice and stir. Strain into a frosted martini glass and garnish with a cocktail onion.

gimlet

A great litmus test for a bar's cocktail capability – too much lime and the drink turns sickly, not enough and the drink is too strong. This one needs to be shaken hard to ensure a sharp freezing zestiness.

25 ml /1 oz. Rose's lime cordial

50 ml/2 oz. gin or vodka

Add both the ingredients to a shaker filled with ice, shake hard and strain through a sieve into a frosted martini glass.

churchill martini

(ALSO KNOWN AS THE NAKED MARTINI)

Winston Churchill, like many of his contemporaries, would search for ways to prevent his beloved martini being sabotaged by the inclusion of too much vermouth. So, whereas some just aromatize their martini with vermouth and others marinade their olives in vermouth, Churchill would merely look at the bottle when fixing himself a martini.

75 ml/3 oz. gin

1 bottle dry vermouth

a green olive, to garnish

Using a mixing glass, chill a large shot of gin over ice and pour into a frosted martini glass. (An easier method is to keep a bottle of gin in the freezer.) Pass a bottle of vermouth over the drink, ensuring that the sun shines through the liquid onto the martini. Garnish with a green olive.

vesper

Named by James Bond in the film *Casino Royale* – Bond christened the drink he devised after his Bond girl de-jour Vesper Lynd. A shaken, medium-dry concoction.

60 ml/2½ oz. gin
20 ml/1 oz. vodka
10 ml/½ oz. Kina Lillet (French vermouth)
a long lemon peel, to garnish

Add all the ingredients to shaker filled with ice, shake and strain into a frosted martini glass. Garnish with the lemon peel and serve.

the ultimate

Every martini should be made using the very finest components. Make this martini the 'ultimate' by choosing from the exceptional quality spirits now available.

1 drop Vya dry vermouth

50 ml/2 oz. freezing ultra premium gin or vodka

a twist of lemon or a green olive, to garnish

Rinse a frosted martini glass with the vermouth and discard. Add the spirit and garnish with a twist of lemon or an olive.

the personaltini

As a lover of martinis of all shapes and sizes, it wasn't easy to name my favourite but here it is. A naked black Stoli martini, stirred and served up. Create and name your own martini.

60 ml/2¹/₂ oz. Stolichnaya vodka

a black olive, to garnish

Add the Stoli vodka to a mixing glass filled with ice, stir until the mixing glass frosts and strain into a frosted martini glass. Garnish with a black olive.

horse's

This recipe stems from the days when gin and vodka were considered medicinal. The ginger would have been added not only to flavour the elixir, but also to act as a herbal remedy to cure most ills.

12.5 ml/¹/₂ oz. ginger liqueur
50 ml/2 oz. vodka
a whole lemon peel, to garnish

Add both ingredients to a shaker filled with ice, shake sharply and strain into a frosted martini glass. Garnish with a whole lemon peel.

martinez

The Martinez is believed to be the first documented martini, dating back as far as 1849 when it was mixed for a miner who had just struck gold in the town of Martinez, California. Its sweet flavours were geared to appeal to the taste buds of the time and the availability of certain spirits.

50 ml/2 oz. Old Tom Gin

12.5 ml/½ oz. sweet vermouth

a dash of orange bitters

a dash of maraschino

a lemon twist, to garnish

Add all the ingredients to a shaker filled with ice, shake and strain into a frosted martini glass. Garnish with a lemon twist.

fresh
& fruity

watermelon martini

Once London's bartenders discovered that using the juice of ripe, preferably tropical, fruit in cocktails was eminently more desirable than using vodka infused with jelly beans and chocolate, their creativity was unbounded.

a slice of watermelon plus a small wedge of melon, to garnish

50 ml /2 oz. vodka

a dash of sugar syrup

Put the chopped flesh of the watermelon in a shaker, crush it slightly then add ice, the vodka and a hint of sugar syrup to taste. Shake the mixture sharply and strain into a frosted martini glass. Garnish with a small wedge of watermelon.

breakfast martini

This pretty much says it all for the versatility of vodka and the extremes to which bartenders will go to create something new and off the wall. It's not a drink that I would recommend to accompany your cornflakes, unless first thing in the morning is actually last thing at night for you. If you fancy something a little more tangy, try replacing the orange marmalade with lime marmalade.

50 ml/2 oz. vodka

25 ml/1 oz. lemon juice

25 ml/1 oz. Cointreau

2 barspoons marmalade

Pour the vodka, lemon juice and Cointreau into a shaker filled with ice, add the marmalade, shake sharply and strain into a frosted martini glass.

citrus

Another old favourite, the citrus needs to be shaken hard to take the edge off the lemon. Try substituting lime for lemon for a slightly more tart variation.

50 ml/2 oz. Cytrynowka vodka
25 ml/1 oz. lemon juice
25 ml/1 oz. Cointreau
a dash of sugar syrup
a lemon zest, to garnish

Add all the ingredients to a shaker filled with ice, shake sharply and strain into a frosted martini glass. Garnish with the lemon zest.

metropolitan

This cocktail was one of the originals on the Met Bar menu. It uses one of the more creditable flavours of the vodkas in Absolut's arsenal with great success. The blackcurrant vodka, combined with the cranberry and balanced by the lime juice makes for quite a fruity concoction. It's very difficult to be entirely sure of the origin of any cocktail, all I know is that this one appeared on my menu in 1998.

50 ml/2 oz. Absolut Kurant Vodka

25 ml/1 oz. triple sec

25 ml/1 oz. fresh lime juice

25 ml/1 oz. cranberry juice

an orange zest, to garnish

Shake all the ingredients sharply over ice and strain into a frosted martini glass. Squeeze the oil from a strip of orange zest, skin downwards over a flame, held over the glass. Rub the rim with the orange zest before dropping it into the glass.

blood martini

A bittersweet concoction that needs to be delicately balanced. The lime and the Campari provide the bitterness, while the sweet element comes in the form of the raspberry liqueur. Taste the drink before and after adding the orange zest – what a difference!

50 ml/2 oz. vodka

15 ml/1 tablespoon Campari

10 ml/2 barspoons framboise

5 ml/1 barspoon fresh lime juice

25 ml/1 oz. cranberry juice

a dash of Cointreau

a flaming orange zest, to garnish

Add all the ingredients to a shaker filled with ice, shake sharply and strain into a frosted martini glass. Garnish with a flaming orange zest (see page 9)

raspberry

The Raspberry is an old favourite of mine. This martini should be fairly thick in consistency, so if you aren't using purée, use a handful of raspberries to make sure it flows down your throat like molasses.

50 ml/2 oz. vodka

a dash of framboise

a dash of orange bitters

12.5 ml/1/2 oz. raspberry purée

2 fresh raspberries, to garnish

Shake all the ingredients in a shaker filled with ice and strain into a frosted martini glass. Garnish with the fresh raspberries.

pontberry

The Pontberry martini is a snip to prepare since it involves no fresh fruit. Strong and sweet, it should appeal to a wide range of palates.

50 ml/2 oz. vodka

75 ml/3 oz. cranberry juice

a large dash of crème de mure

Shake all the ingredients in a shaker filled with ice. Strain into a frosted martini glass and serve.

cherry

This martini can also be made using the juice from canned cherries – it may not sound as nice on paper but wait until you taste it. For a delicious variation, try using the juice from canned lychees – another winner!

3 pitted fresh cherries

50 ml/2 oz. vodka

50 ml/2 oz. thick cherry juice

a dash of cherry schnapps

Crush the cherries in a shaker. Add ice and the remaining ingredients, shake sharply, and strain through a sieve into a frosted martini glass.

pear

This fruit martini is certainly not for the faint-hearted. Unlike a lot of the fruit martinis whose sweetness belies their strength, this one pulls no punches.

50 ml/2 oz. vodka
a dash of Poire Williams eau de vie
a thin pear slice, to garnish

Shake all the ingredients in a shaker filled with ice and strain through a sieve into a frosted martini glass. Garnish with a thin slice of pear and serve.

kiwi martini

The fruit used should be as ripe and fresh as possible; the dash of sugar mentioned in the recipes is only to sweeten unripe fruit.

1 fresh kiwi fruit

50 ml/2 oz. vodka

a dash of sugar syrup

Crush a peeled, sliced ripe kiwi fruit in a shaker (reserving a slice to garnish), using a muddler or the flat end of a barspoon. Add ice, the measure of vodka and sugar syrup to taste. Shake and strain into a frosted martini glass. Garnish with a slice of kiwi fruit.

pomegranate

As this is one of the subtler of the fruit martinis, care must be taken to ensure the pomegranate is ripe. Try to avoid getting any of the fruit's bitter pith in the drink, as this would destroy its delicate balance.

50 ml/2 oz. vodka

1 pomegranate

a dash of sugar syrup

pomegranate seeds, to garnish

Spoon the pomegranate 'flesh' into a shaker and crush, using a muddler or the flat end of a barspoon. Add ice to the shaker with the remaining ingredients. Shake sharply and strain through a sieve into a frosted martini glass. Garnish with a few pomegranate seeds.

applejack

Taken from recipes using American apple brandy, this concoction relies heavily on the addition of Manzana, a green apple liqueur that lends a bitter-sweet quality to the martini.

25 ml/1 oz. vodka

25 ml/1 oz. Manzana apple liqueur

20 ml/1 scant oz. Calvados

a thin slice of green apple, to garnish

Add all the ingredients to a mixing glass filled with ice, stir until the glass appears frosted and strain into a frosted martini glass. Garnish with a thin slice of apple.

french

The French martini is great for parties as it is light and creamy, and simple to make in bulk. Shake this one hard when preparing it and you will be rewarded with a thick white froth on the surface of the drink.

50 ml/2 oz. vodka

a large dash of Chambord

   (or crème de mure)

75 ml/3 oz. fresh pineapple juice

Add all the ingredients to a shaker filled with ice, shake sharply and strain into a frosted martini glass.

strawberry

Use the ripest strawberries in this martini. The strawberry flavour is enhanced by a dash of fraise (strawberry liqueur), but this should be kept to a minimum compared to the fresh fruit.

3 fresh strawberries

2 barspoons sugar syrup

50 ml/2 oz. vodka

a dash of crème de fraise

Place the strawberries into a shaker and muddle with the flat end of a barspoon. Add the remaining ingredients, shake hard and strain through a sieve into a frosted martini glass.

basil grande

One of the few martinis that doesn't use vodka or gin exclusively as the base, so expect lots of strong flavours in this extravagantly fruity concoction. It's a great alternative to creamy cocktails after dinner.

4 strawberries (one to garnish)

3 basil leaves (one to garnish)

25 ml/1 oz. Grand Marnier

25 ml/1 oz. vodka

25 ml/1 oz. Chambord (or crème de mure)

50 ml/2 oz. cranberry juice

Crush the strawberries and two basil leaves in a shaker. Add the remaining ingredients with ice, shake sharply and strain through a sieve into a frosted martini glass. Garnish with a strawberry and a basil leaf.

clean
& serene

sapphire martini

This is an amazingly simple variation on the martini. Bombay Sapphire gin, with its spicy notes, is the perfect match for the Parfait d'Amour. Although unpromising on its own, a couple of drops of the very blue Parfait d'Amour combined with well chilled Bombay Sapphire Gin produces a magnificent cocktail.

a dash of Parfait d'Amour

50 ml/2 oz. Bombay Sapphire Gin

blueberries, to garnish

Gently pour the Parfait d'Amour into a frosted martini glass. Over a barspoon, pour the gin (which should have been in the freezer for at least 1 hour) so that it sits over the blue liqueur. Garnish with blueberries on a cocktail stick.

azure martini

Cachaça, a spirit indigenous to Brazil is distilled directly from the juice of sugar cane, unlike rum, which is usually distilled from molasses. The Caipirinha has made cachaça popular in many countries.

1/2 an apple

50 ml/2 oz. cachaça

12.5 ml/1/2 oz. canella liqueur

a dash of fresh lime or lemon juice

a dash of sugar syrup

Pound the apple in the bottom of a cocktail shaker to release the flavour. Add crushed ice and the remaining ingredients, shake and strain through a sieve into a frosted martini glass.

gotham

As sinister and mysterious as the name
suggests. Try varying the amount of
black Sambuca for a darker, more
threatening result.

60 ml/2¹/₂ oz. frozen Stolichnaya vodka

a dash of black Sambuca

Pour the vodka into a frosted martini glass,
gently add the Sambuca, and serve.

the journalist

I've never been a supporter of unnecessarily complicated cocktails but this one seems to succeed against all the odds. The Journalist defies convention but is great as a palate-cleansing aperitif. The sweet/dry theme is repeated twice, with the sweet and dry vermouth, then the triple sec and lemon juice. Definitely a good pre-dinner drink to order at a bar, but if you are making it at home watch the measurements carefully; it's a drink that needs to be very finely balanced.

25 ml/1 oz. gin

a dash of sweet vermouth

a dash of dry vermouth

2 dashes of fresh lemon juice

2 dashes of triple sec

2 dashes of Angostura bitters

Shake all the ingredients over ice and strain into a frosted martini glass.

sake martini

The Sake Martini uses the heady combination of gin, vodka and sake, which might not sound very tempting, but take it from me, it's definitely worth having a try next time you order that takeaway sushi!

25 ml/1 oz. sake

25 ml/1 oz. vodka

a dash of gin

a slice of cucumber, to garnish

Pour the sake, vodka and a dash of gin into a mixing glass filled with ice. Stir the mixture until thoroughly chilled and strain into a frosted martini glass. Garnish with a slice of cucumber.

thunderer

This cocktail smells almost perfumed.
A hint of Parfait d'Amour – a beautifully
named orange curaçao flavoured with
violets – and a tease of cassis is all this
drink needs to achieve its flowery,
distinctive taste.

60 ml/2¹/₂ oz. frozen vodka

2 drops of Parfait d'Amour

2 drops of cassis

2 blueberries, to garnish

Pour the Parfait d'Amour and cassis into
a frosted martini glass. Add the frozen
vodka and garnish with two blueberries.

polish martini

The Polish Martini combines the bitterness
of Zubrowka with the potent sweetness
of Krupnik honey vodka and the crispness
of apple juice, creating a beguiling
depth of taste.

25 ml/1 oz. Zubrowka Vodka
25 ml/1 oz. Krupnik Vodka
25 ml/1 oz. fresh apple juice

Add single shots of Krupnik Vodka,
Zubrowka Vodka and apple juice into a
mixing glass filled with ice. Stir and strain
into a frosted martini glass.

The Bronx dates back to the days of Prohibition, when gang bosses reigned and booze played an important part in the economy of the underworld. Different areas of New York became known for the special cocktails they offered, such as this speciality of the Bronx district. Like the Manhattan, it has three variations: the dry, the sweet and the perfect. The Silver and Golden Bronx are variations on the perfect with the addition of egg white or egg yolk.

silver bronx

50 ml/2 oz. gin

a dash of dry vermouth

a dash of sweet vermouth

50 ml/2 oz. fresh orange juice

1 egg white

Shake all the ingredients vigorously over ice and strain into a chilled cocktail glass.

golden bronx

The method is the same as left, but substitute the egg white for an egg yolk.

joe average

Despite its name, there is nothing average about this drink. Nor should the Pimm's in the recipe fool you – this is not a drink to be taken lightly.

60 ml/2½ oz. Stolichnaya vodka

a dash of Pimm's No 1 cup

a thin slice of cucumber and a lemon zest, to garnish

Add the ingredients to a mixing glass filled with ice, stir until the glass appears frosted and strain into a frosted martini glass. Garnish with a thin slice of cucumber and lemon zest.

decadent

cheesecake

You'll need a spoon with this one —
it's effectively an alcoholic dessert.

a digestive biscuit/graham cracker
10 ml/2 barspoons sugar syrup
50 ml/2 oz. vodka
12.5 ml/1/2 oz. Chambord
12.5 ml/1/2 oz. raspberry purée
12.5 ml/1/2 oz. double/heavy cream

Grind the biscuit/cracker into crumbs, add the
sugar syrup, mix and pack into the bottom of
a martini glass. Add the remaining ingredients
in to a shaker, shake and strain gently over the
crumbs into the martini glass.

orange brûlée

The Orange Brûlée is a dessert drink that should be savoured. You'll notice I don't recommend the caramelization process – would you trust a bartender with a blowtorch?

25 ml/1 oz. Grand Marnier

12.5 ml/$\frac{1}{2}$ oz. Amaretto

a dash of white crème de cacao

whipping cream, to top

thin strips of orange zest, to garnish

Add all the ingredients (except the cream) to a shaker filled with ice, shake sharply and strain into a martini glass. Whip the cream and dollop gently over the surface of the drink. Criss-cross with orange zest.

lemon meringue

When set the challenge to create something special with Drambuie Cream, I thought I'd bend the rules a little. Mixing citrus fruits with cream liqueurs generally isn't recommended for cocktails, but somehow this concoction resists the temptation to curdle.

50 ml/2 oz. Cytrynowka vodka

20 ml/4 barspoons lemon juice

12.5 ml/½ oz. Drambuie Cream

a dash of sugar syrup

Add all the ingredients to a shaker filled with ice, shake sharply and strain into a frosted martini glass.

chocolate mint martini

The Chocolate Martini was a great discovery, with a dash of white crème de cacao, it saved bartenders from trying to create the chocolate taste by forcing Mars Bars into bottles of vodka!

50 ml/2 oz. vodka

25 ml/1 oz. crème de cacao (white)

12.5 ml/¹/₂ oz. crème de menthe (white)

Into a shaker filled with ice, pour the vodka, the crème de cacao and the crème de menthe. Shake and strain into a frosted martini glass with a cocoa rim.

turkish chocolate martini

I've always wanted to find a credible drink that includes rose-flower water; and here it is. The heaviness of the crème de cacao combines with the lightness of the flower water to create a truly Turkish delight.

50 ml/2 oz. vodka

10 ml/2 barspoons crème de cacao (light)

2 dashes of rose-flower water

cocoa powder (for the rim)

Add all the ingredients to a shaker filled with ice, shake and strain into a frosted martini glass with a cocoa rim.

hazelnut

This martini has proven to be popular with men and women alike. A strong, clear chocolate martini with an undercurrent of hazelnut, perfect for after dinner with a coffee – dessert and a nightcap rolled into one.

50 ml/2 oz. vodka

20 ml/4 barspoons crème de cacao (light)

10 ml/2 barspoons Frangelico (hazelnut liqueur)

ground nutmeg (for the rim)

Add all the ingredients to a shaker filled with ice, shake and strain into a frosted martini glass with a nutmeg rim.

black bison

The central ingredient to this mix is Zubrowka, a vodka that tastes of freshly cut hay, and lends a distinct quality to any cocktail. Combine this with Chambord (a black raspberry liqueur from the Loire Valley) and you have a truly memorable union.

50 ml/2 oz. Zubrowka vodka

20 ml/4 barspoons Chambord (or crème de mure)

12.5 ml/½ oz. fresh lime juice

a dash of sugar syrup

4 blackcurrants

a blueberry, to garnish

Muddle the blackcurrants in a shaker. Add the remaining ingredients to the shaker with ice, shake sharply and strain into a frosted martini glass. Garnish with a blueberry.

herbed
& spiced

red star

The Red Star is a delicate drink. Ensure
the glass is well frosted to highlight the
hint of aniseed taken from the seed of
this Chinese plant.

50 ml/2 oz. vodka

*15 ml/1 tablespoon star anise-infused
   dry vermouth**

4 star anise (one to garnish)

Add the dry vermouth and the vodka to a
mixing glass filled with ice and stir until the
glass is frosted. Strain into a frosted martini
glass and garnish with a star anise.

* Infuse three star anise into a bottle of
vermouth (Noilly Prat) for two days.

lemongrass

A gentle hint of lemongrass is all that
is required for this concoction to work. Try
this martini before sitting down to a Thai meal.
The lemongrass skirt in the photo is not a recommended
garnish (unless you have a degree in basket weaving.)

60 ml/2¹/₂ oz. lemon grass-infused vodka*

3 sticks of lemongrass (one to garnish)

Add the vodka to a mixing glass filled with ice, stir until the
glass is frosted and strain into a frosted martini glass. Garnish
with a thin slice of lemongrass.

* Place two split lemongrass sticks into a bottle of vodka and
leave to infuse for two days.

elderflower

Elderflower cordial has become a must-have on bar shelves in recent years – try this recipe with gin instead of vodka as a base and marvel as the juniper and other flavourings in the gin combine with the sweet elderflower!

50 ml/2 oz. vodka

25 ml/1 oz. lime juice

12.5 ml/1/2 oz. elderflower cordial

a dash of sugar syrup

a dash of orange bitters

a lime zest, to garnish

Add all the ingredients to a mixing glass filled with ice, stir until the glass is frosted and strain into a frosted martini glass. Garnish with a lime zest.

hibiscus

It's always worth experimenting with the Hibiscus before you serve it to your guests, as the concentration of the juice can vary – overdo the hibiscus if in doubt.

25 ml/1 oz. vodka

a dash of lime juice

a dash of framboise liqueur

50 ml/2 oz. hibiscus cordial*

an hibiscus flower or petal, to garnish

Add all the ingredients to a shaker filled with ice, shake sharply and strain into a frosted martini glass. Garnish with an hibiscus flower.

*Dissolve 500g/2 cups sugar and 100 g/3¹/₂ oz. hibiscus flower (dried if out of season) into 2 litres/8 cups of water on a low heat. Once the liquid turns a deep red, strain and leave to cool.

tokyo

This martini can be a bit of a scary one if made badly. Try to find the best quality wasabi and the freshest ginger.

50 ml/2 oz. gin

2 thin strips of fresh ginger

a small roll of wasabi

ginger strip, to garnish

Add the ingredients to a shaker filled with ice, shake and strain into a frosted martini glass. Garnish with a thin strip of ginger.

cowboy hoof

Who knows where the name for this minty special originates! The colour of the drink alone is worth the effort. Do pay attention when straining the mixture as bits of mint sticking to the teeth is never a good look.

12 mint leaves

2 barspoons sugar syrup

65 ml/2¹/₂ oz. gin

a sprig of fresh mint, to garnish

Shake all the ingredients in a shaker filled with ice and strain through a sieve into a frosted martini glass. Garnish with a sprig of fresh mint.

cajun

A word of warning, this drink must be monitored while it is infusing. Habañero chillies are incredibly strong and should be treated with respect. A glass of milk will neutralize the effect if you over-do it!

60 ml/2¹/₂ oz. habañero-infused vodka*
4 habañero chillies (one to garnish)

Add the vodka to a mixing glass filled with ice and stir until the glass is frosted. Strain into a frosted martini glass and garnish with a habañero chilli.

* Place three habañero chillies (with seeds) into a bottle of vodka and leave until they start to loose their colour (the more translucent the chillies become, the more flavour has been absorbed in to the vodka).

INDEX